P*rom* P*assions*

**A Young Woman's Guide
To Her Best Night Ever**

J**oy**
S**ingleton**

xulon PRESS

Prom Passions
by Joy Singleton

Printed in the United States of America

ISBN 1-60034-157-8

Unless otherwise indicated, Bible quotations are taken from the New International Version. Copyright © 1973, 1978, 1984 by International Bible Society.

www.xulonpress.com

*D*edication

*To every young woman
who wants more for her life*

Acknowledgements

They infused my life with their words...

So many people have poured into my life and for that I'm grateful! As it relates to this project, there are a few who must be acknowledged for helping birth this book. Deborah Anderson, you were the first to declare I was destined to write books; thank you for believing it with all your heart. Rev. Terri McFaddin, you spoke this book into existence; thank you for the walk in the canyon and your prophetic impartation. Cornell Fields, your commitment to seeing me walk out this process has renewed my focus and strength many days.

Nicole Kelly, Staci Singleton and Dekia Smith, your faith and feedback have been invaluable. I thank every student that gave constructive feedback, especially Drina Duryea, Chelsea Persons, Janelle Van Siclen, Amanda Shaffer and Nikita Taparia. Larry H.

Lyons, thank you, thank you, thank you for editing this book amid Ph.D exams.

Bishop Donald Hilliard, Jr. and Dr. Bernadette Glover-Williams, you have been constant examples of excellence, holiness and dream fulfillment. Your best is yet to come!

Table Of Contents

*I*ntroduction

Deep within the heart of every young woman are hidden caverns filled with secret thoughts, overflowing joys, burdensome pains and unknown regions that impact the way she views and experiences the world. She needs time and space to excavate, and thus understand and appreciate the full value of the hidden treasures preserved within. *Prom Passions* journeys with the female teen to discover her true prom desires and gives her tools and skills to make wiser choices for her exciting night.

Prom Passions helps every young woman answer questions like: How can I make all my prom dreams come true? How far is too far? And how can I have a good time at prom without going against my conscience? Since teenagers experience so much emotionally, sexually and spiritually, there is no topic too taboo for *Prom Passions* to handle—young women live in a real world and face genuine issues of concern. Thus, this book boldly speaks the language of today's youth and is unapologetically real.

Yet, there is something in this book for everyone! Whether the reader is in junior high or high school, **Prom Passions** just might make her laugh hysterically, ponder seriously and change permanently for the better.

Each chapter is intentionally unique, having its own topic, characters and stylistic presentation. This layout allows the reader to skip around as necessary, without missing important pieces of information.

Six chapters include special sections:

*_My Prom Passions_ is like a personal journal where the reader can reflect on questions that will help her discover her heart's desires concerning prom night.

*_For Young Women Who Want More_ challenges the young female to face the heart of the matter. Straightforward and very candid, this section is designed for mature, young women.

So, enjoy your journey through **Prom Passions;** in the end, your best night will become reality!

Chapter 1

A Night to Remember

Nikki:

"Uuuuh…oooh…" Thump! Wrapped in her sweat-drenched sheet like a mummy, Nikki struggled to unravel herself.

"Where's the toilet?" she would have mumbled, but her pulsating head throb and the churning noise from her stomach kept her brain from putting the words in order. She was so messed up, she didn't realize she was in her own bedroom. Eyes wide-squinted, Nikki gripped the floor as the room spun faster than an amusement park ride. "Hey, this isn't fair!" Nikki thought, as she searched to find the conductor of the ride she seemed to be on.

Everything was fuzzy. Taunted by mirages of her so-called friends encouraging her to guzzle down the different enticing, sweet umbrella drinks laced with alcohol, Nikki was fed up, "Guys, this isn't funny anymore!" Wondering what happened last night, she found her way out of the sheet and slowly crawled in the direction she thought the door would be. "Ooooh, I feel horrible…"

Flush.

"Aaaaah!" Nikki sighed, as she became best friends with the white and orange splattered toilet bowl. The fragrance of the air spray wasn't strong enough to cover the potency of her vomit.

Held up by the strength of the pea green wall, Nikki put one foot in front of the other and ended up back in her room. Her prom attire was strewn everywhere: dress crumpled at the door, stockings dangling from the lampshade, jewelry in pieces on the floor, bra hanging from the bed canopy and underwear on her desk. Seeing her room in complete disarray, Nikki realized for the first time that she was naked. Suddenly, both hands clamped her mouth to stifle the unnerving scream springing forth from her newly relieved belly. Who was that guy in her bed?!? Nikki tried not to panic, but she couldn't remember who the guy was, when they had returned to her parents' house or what they had done. "I've got to get him out of here!"

Aaliyah:

Her younger sister, Tasha, couldn't wait for Aaliyah to wake up. She had stayed up half the night with a flashlight, her secret journal and two pink pens trying to capture every question she wanted to ask

Aaliyah when she finally opened her eyes. Aaliyah dreamily turned over, only to be startled by her anxious sister staring in her face.

"Alright, so what happened A'?" abruptly ending Aaliyah's continual replay of the best night of her life.

Reveling in the fulfillment of her prom dream, Aaliyah sleepily propped herself up on the closest pillow. Where should she begin? Her sister jumped in her bed, ready to hear every detail. Comfortable now, Aaliyah leaned back to recount her unforgettable night:

"Well, as you know, it all started with that fire-hot, white limo and the shiny rims. Steve opened the door for me and the limo was plushed out! The driver took us to Tanya's and John was already there. Her backyard was perfect for pictures, with beautiful pink and white flowers falling from the trees. Everything was right! We went to the Manor and when we pulled up, Steve took my hand and helped me out the limo. There was a red carpet, lights and pictures snapping everywhere. Steve was the finest brotha' there and I KNOW I was the prettiest girl in the place...

We had fun the w-h-o-l-e night! All of my friends were there and we laughed, ate, danced and wild out together. It was like all the drama that had gone on during the school year was squashed. Bobbie and LeDaran didn't fight and Falita and Fatima didn't get into it — you know Falita stole Fatima's man a few months ago. Girl, Fatima has been trippin' ever since--I don't know why she keeps sweatin' Mike.

Anyway, Tamara had an after-party at her house and we all went there and bugged out! The music was off the chain! Everybody danced and you know it was hot up in there. Tamara's cousin taught us a game and we played for about 2 hours. And you know how *we* do: after all that dancing and game playing, we went to the diner and got our grub on!

The night ended with Steve opening the door for me and walking me up to the porch… That's my boo! He surprised me with a pink rose and a card, thanking me for…"

"Did he kiss you?" Tasha needed to know before the story went any further. "Well, did he?"

Throwing her arms around her younger sister and squeezing, Aaliyah quickly changed the subject, "You know, Tasha, I really need to get back to sleep. We can go through the rest of those questions — how many questions did you write down? We can finish talking later, ok?" Aaliyah simultaneously pulled the comforter up and slouched back down into dream position.

"Come on, "A'!" Did Steve kiss you?" The silence was almost unbearable. Aaliyah's sister sat on the edge of the bed leaning in closer to hear the response.

"Yeah!" Aaliyah beamed.

"Aaaaa! I knew it!" Tasha screamed, smiling as she imagined the fine brotha who would kiss her on the porch on her prom night.

"Girls, quiet down, your step-dad has to go to work in a few hours!" Mom whispered loudly up the stairs.

"Ok, Mom!" they yelled back in chorus.

"And the greatest thing about it was that he didn't rub on me, you know? Some guys try to touch on your butt or your breasts while they kiss you. Steve didn't do any of that. He just kissed me…long and sl-o-o-o-w…it was so sweet!" Aaliyah cheesed, smiling at the memory.

"I can't wait until I can go to the prom!"

Sarah:

Ring!!

"It can't be morning already." Flashes of blurred, slightly-familiar pictures moved in slow motion across the back of Sarah's eyelids. What time was it?

Attempting to keep the merciless sun and the irritating phone ring from piercing her half-awake, half-sleep state, Sarah pulled her other pillow over her head. Shocked by what she saw when her eyes were closed, she abruptly sat up, "What was *that?*!? I don't know how Cindy handled seeing five other girls wearing her dress. Was the dress on sale or what?!?"

A full-body-shaking yawn brought back clearer pictures. "Oh, Felicia is *never* going to recover from that fiasco! What girl can have a good time at the prom when her parents are there dancing with her friends like it's *their* prom? There had even been a circle around them at one point on the dance floor. What were they thinking? Obviously, they weren't! I feel bad for Felicia—they stayed the entire time. How embarrassing!"

"Did I see Mr. Smith playing in Ms. Jenkins' hair? Oh-my-gosh!" Now those flashes were coming in faster. Mr. Smith, the playboy Drama teacher had attended the prom with Sarah's computer teacher. "What was Mr. Smith doing with Ms. Jenkins?" Sarah couldn't remember any lunch gossip and school rumors about Mr. Smith and Ms. Jenkins being an item. How did that one slip by her?

Brian "The Man" Karnegy couldn't dodge Sarah's critique either. Almost fully conscious now, Sarah jumped out the bed, "Wait--what was Brian doing?" He was at the prom with two dates, as if no one would notice he spent half the night at the table in the corner and the other half in the lobby. "He's ridiculous!"

The enticing smell of breakfast reached her nostrils and Sarah looked forward to sinking her teeth into a garden omelet, a warm cinnamon-raisin bagel, two slices of soy bacon and a glass of orange juice. The sound of her annoying brother became unbearable, so she sank back into her bed for a few more minutes of beauty rest.

Ring!

"It's too early to be awake!" Reluctantly drifting back into slow motion pictures, Sarah didn't want to think too much or talk too much about her time at the prom. "He didn't even show up...I saw Aaliyah and her friends having so much fun and even Nikki and her crew seemed to have a good time. I wish someone would've asked me to dance—at least once..." Sarah welcomed the silence that rushed in, but the depression that came along had not been invited. "It doesn't matter," she tried to console herself, "he was such a loser anyway."

Sarah tried to ignore the moisture that had gathered in her left eye to form a trail of tears. "What's wrong with me?" she questioned herself. "I wish I had real friends like the other girls...I don't need that many friends anyhow; they're all just jealous of me!"

Ring!

"Would someone get the phone?!!"

Prom Dreams

For the next few days, all these girls talked about were their prom experiences. People kept asking about their dresses, hairdos, dates, transportation, pictures, the actual prom, and their after-prom activities.

In all the times of re-telling, embellishing and concealing particular parts of their stories, there was one thing these girls had in common: prom memories. All of the detailed plans, trips to the malls and choices they made had worked together to produce the memories each of them would have on the morning after the prom and for the rest of their lives. They didn't know it, but everything they chose to do in preparation for the prom (and after-prom activities) determined the kind of night they remembered.

Nikki:

I didn't want my morning after the prom to be filled with panic, but it was. It took me thirty minutes to figure out who that guy was in my bed. I tried calling friends and whispering so the guy wouldn't wake up. It took five phone calls before I knew his identity, because every person I called was totally stoned and hadn't made her way to the toilet bowl yet. I found out his name is Eric Carpenter and he went to the prom with my friend, Cindy.

Slowly, I began to piece things together. My "friends" and I went to a club for an after-party and we partied hard. We only had to be seventeen to get in and they weren't checking IDs. The bar served these cute drinks with little umbrellas in them. They were so good! They had some alcohol in them, but I thought I could handle it.

After the first two, I felt a buzz that was kind of cool. Even after my fourth drink, my friends encouraged me to drink more. Then I remember the whole club got really loud and rowdy. People were competing to see how many drinks they could hold down. By the sixth, I started to feel sick, so I knocked glass seven out of my friend's hand as she pushed it up to my mouth.

My "friends" and I decided to leave the club and rent a hotel room. We continued the party and took it to the next level by switching partners. Jessica hooked up with my date, Bobbie; I ended up with Eric. There were six couples all together and as the night became morning, newly paired couples started to split up to do their own thing. Eric and I decided not to get a hotel room, but to go back to my house. I don't know how we got there because we were both smashed, but somehow we made it to my bedroom without waking anyone up.

When I shook Eric awake, I didn't even have to ask him if we had had sex together. I felt it in my body and smelled it in the air. His first words were, "Baby, Cindy never told me you were a freak. Let's do it again!" He started pulling me close to him, but I pushed him away and told him he had to get out my house. While he searched around and pulled his clothes on, I couldn't help wondering if he had used a condom. So I asked him and he said, "No way, Baby; I like it natural."

Drinking until I lost my mind? That wasn't quite my intention and I didn't start out saying that my prom night was going to be about sleeping with a guy I didn't know, but that's how it ended. I woke up the next morning sick as a dog wondering if I had caught any fleas! We were all lucky to make it home because all of us had been drinking. I wasn't thinking about it then, but any of us could have died driving home! And the sex...I don't even remember it. I do know Eric never talked to Cindy again and Cindy stopped speaking to me. Out of all of my friends, I'm the only one that ended up pregnant. I still have a few weeks to decide whether or not I'm going to keep this baby.

All I really wanted for my prom memories were thoughts of having a good time with my friends. What I have been left with, though, are taunting images, broken friendships and a swollen belly. Yeah, it was a night I can't help but to remember.

Aaliyah:

I expected my little sister, Tasha, to ask me about my prom, but she was ridiculous! I mean, the second I turned over--bam--she was in my grill bombarding me with questions. My prom went exactly as I pictured it—actually, it was better.

I made sure that everything was set. Steve and I talked about what we wanted for our prom and we both agreed on having a good time with our friends and each other. Oh, Steve knew I wasn't having all of that drinking and rubbing and stuff. I wanted to be sober and I didn't want to be in a position I couldn't get myself out of. So, we played it safe, but not corny. We had the time of our lives!

Now, to be honest, I wanted to hug and kiss, but I didn't want us to regret anything. The kiss...At first we were cool and then we really got into it. It was like we were in a completely different galaxy for awhile. His lips were so soft and luscious! I will always remember them. When we came back to the reality of being on my porch and my father waiting up for me on the other side of the door, he pulled out the rose and the card. I thought he was going to hand it to me, give me an abbreviated kiss and get in his car. Instead, he took my hand.

I don't know where he found the words, but Steve looked me in my eyes and thanked me so poetically for being his perfect date, for making his prom one *of the greatest nights of his life. I didn't know until then that he had always wanted to ask me out, but had been too shy until needing a date for the prom presented the opportunity. We hung out a few times after school ended. He's the kind of guy a girl likes to keep, you know? I couldn't have asked for a better night: it's one I always want to remember.*

Sarah:

You want to know what memories I had planned for my prom night? I wanted to be the Prom Queen, but I didn't win because everyone is jealous of me. I see the look in the other girls' eyes. They despise me. My date was the star football player at my school. I don't know why he asked me to the prom, but it put me in perfect position to win the prom queen title.

I envisioned us walking across the stage with our royal crowns and sashes, everyone envying us as the "Couple of the Night." I had even practiced my queen wave and bleached my teeth for the perfect-white smile.

Actually, I convinced the few friends I have to bribe him to take me, promising that I was willing to do anything he wanted me to—naughty or nice. Everything was going according to plan until he didn't show up to the prom. What nerve! He wasn't worth my time of day, anyway, with his inability to multiply and divide fractions. What an idiot!

Those tears? I don't know where they came from. Sometimes I wish I didn't have to bribe people to be my friends. I wanted to have a great prom night like everyone else, but I ruined it with deception and lies. I really wanted him to ask me out, not because of unmentionable promises, but because he saw something special in me. My friends didn't even show up to the prom because they were fed up with me. They said they were tired of me talking about other people and never noticing how mean and spiteful I could be...I knew they were right.

I sat there all night watching others enjoy the festivities and all I could do was pick out what was wrong with everyone else so I didn't have to focus on what wasn't right with me. I didn't picture a night of criticizing people, but that's what it turned out to be when I got through. A night to remember? Yeah, but I'd actually prefer to forget it.

My Prom Passions: How Will My Night Be Remembered?

1. On prom night, I expect to:

2. How realistic are my expectations?

3. When I awake the morning after my prom, what memories do I want to have?

4. What decisions do I need to make in order for my prom dreams to come true?

5. What consequences may I have to deal with because of the kind of prom experiences I want and the decisions I'll make?

6. How can those consequences affect me, my life now and my life in the future?

—*For Young Women Who Want More*—

Sometimes there's a major gap between what we target and the mark we actually hit. For instance, we say we want to have fun, but many times the activities we deem "fun" don't deliver pure fun at all:

it's not fun throwing up after consuming too much alcohol, awaiting test results to confirm whether or not you've contracted a disease or wrestling with the decisions that come with being a pregnant teen. *Pure fun is enjoyable from the beginning to the last consequence.*

We tend to think happiness comes with doing what we want to do now and dealing with consequences later. That line of thinking is expressed when we stay out with a boyfriend beyond curfew, skip homework assignments to hang with friends or cut school, knowing we'll have to face repercussions. We often think "If _____ would just _____ __, I'd be happy" or "_____ would make me happy." Is it true, lasting happiness? No. There is an enjoyment that comes from being ourselves, making smart choices and caring about ourselves, that isn't based on anyone or anything else. There's no replacement for being happy with who you are. *Real happiness comes from loving and being comfortable with yourself*—even if that means going against the accepted and expected norms of your peers.

Fun and happiness have been redefined; so now, let's consider freedom. We usually think freedom is *being able to do anything I want, when, how and with whom I want*. That definition gets expressed through speed racing down a winding road, experimenting with Ecstasy or having sex with a boy who expresses an interest. Living that kind of life results in us becoming driven by our own desires, unable to think clearly and destroying ourselves. Real freedom, however, is life within boundaries designed to keep us safe, healthy and growing. This freedom is experienced when we choose to protect ourselves from date rape by remaining in public places, study daily to achieve the grades that secure scholarships for college or remain safe by being where we're supposed to be at all times. Making decisions that don't require you to betray your conscience will ultimately provide you a greater sense of personal freedom and satisfaction. *The best use of freedom is to make decisions that will benefit, encourage, protect and give life to yourself and others.*

-A happy heart makes the face cheerful, but heart-ache crushes the spirit.-
Proverb 15: 13

Chapter 2

*D*ollars *a*nd *S*ense

Here's a riddle. Ready?
*What's 2.61 inches wide, 6.14 inches long and so
powerful, people listen when they speak?*
Answer: *Dollar bills!*

You've probably heard someone say, "Money makes the world go round." Well, money can also make decisions for you about what you can and cannot do on your prom night. The reality is you must have money to go to prom. Failing to plan will definitely force you to make choices and compromises you'd rather avoid. Why settle for less? Have a financial prom plan.

Don't Wait

It's crucial to find out EARLY who's going to pay for all your prom expenses. You don't want to find yourself missing out on prom or scrambling at the end to keep your prom dreams from falling apart. Assuming your parents or guardians will pick up the tab may leave you standing outside the prom snapping pictures of others as they happily float into their "Night to Remember." As soon as you know the date for your prom, have a conversation with your parents or guardians about the amount of money you can expect from them for that wonderful day. You may be surprised. Some have been waiting seventeen or eighteen years to pay for your special night!

The earlier you ask, the more time others have to come up with your desired amount. You want as little stress associated with prom as possible. The less stress, the better and the easier the dollar bills will jump out of their hands into yours.

Don't Get It Twisted

You know your parents or guardians better than anyone. This chapter will present different scenarios and possible ways of negotiating with your parents or guardians concerning finances for prom. These scenarios and suggestions may or may not be appropriate or helpful for you. You know what your parents or guardians will agree with and what will get you into trouble. So, don't get it twisted: this chapter is not a step-by-step guide to negotiations, but rather a picture of possibilities. Remember to be honest and straightforward in negotiations because lying and stretching the truth will come back to haunt you.

Phew!

Jumping out of the sturdy kitchen chair and beaming from ear to ear, Kristin squeezed her father's neck so hard he thought his head might pop off! The redness quickly flushed down his face after Kristin released her strong hold. Kristin had hoped her father would agree to pay for everything for prom and "Yes" had been his response. The conversation had gone smoothly, as anticipated. Kristin had simply told her dad that the prom Committee had announced the prom date and theme. She expressed her excitement about attending and let him know that it would be really helpful if he would tell her if he was going to pay for her prom or if she had to find some other means to pay for it. Feeling victorious, Kristin leaped up the stairs to call her other friends to find out how their talk with the parents and guardians had gone.

Negotiations

Unlike Kristin, you might have a more difficult time convincing your parents or guardians to handle the bill for your prom—but don't give up! You may still have some leverage you can use to get all, most or some of your financial prom support. Think of yourself as a lawyer. Know the facts, share the facts and stick to the facts. Some parents or guardians may need a little more convincing than others.

Things You Must Tell Them:

1. When the prom is and how much tickets cost
2. How much you are looking to forward to attending your prom
3. The prom theme
4. How much you appreciate their love and support
5. How you plan to save them money on prom purchases
6. The benefits they'll receive from paying for your prom

Yes, there are benefits your parents or guardians will receive from paying for your prom, such as the joy of making your dreams come true.

If the suggestions above don't seal the deal, buy some time. Tell them, "I know this might sound a bit overwhelming, so why don't you take some time to think about it. We can talk about it again in...two weeks. How does that sound?" They will have their time to think about it and you will sound very considerate. Wise move.

Make sure to mark the two-week date in your planner to ask them if they have come to a decision about paying for your prom. If they haven't made up their minds, give them another week to come up with something conclusive. At the end of that time, if your parents or guardians still haven't decided, or decided to pay less than full, don't fret.

End of Round One

In the heat of battle—well, prom negotiations—
with her mother and step-father, Tracy had almost
broken out into a sweat. They were demanding details
she hadn't been prepared to discuss. Like skilled
boxers they blocked the "sale" and "coupon" promise.
Kristin's phone call had just come through as Tracy's
folks were cracking up at the thought of benefiting
from paying for her prom. It was the perfect inter-
ruption. Sensing it would be a few moments before
they could pull themselves together, they sent Tracy
down the hall to answer her phone. Crunching on her
juicy apple, Kristin jumped right in with her story of
kitchen victory. She carried on so much Tracy had to
press the number two button on the phone to make
her stop talking.

Wiping her brow, Tracy quickly recapped her
conversation and prepared to enter the kitchen for
the next round of negotiations. Her parents hadn't
asked for time to think; they wanted her to do her
best to convince them that they really should pay the
full amount for prom. Taking some last minute tips
from Kristin before hanging up, Tracy headed back
down the hallway for another round. She pictured
herself hearing them say the words, "Ok. We're
sold! You got it, Kido; we'll pay for your prom."
The vision in site, Tracy sat down for round two at
the negotiating table.

Other Things You Must Tell Them:
1. Your good grades and achievements worthy of celebration
2. What you're willing to do in exchange for them paying for prom
3. How special and important the prom is to you
4. How their paying for prom will give you more time to focus on your final exams.

If that doesn't work, take a discrete deep breath. You still have some things working for you.

Timing Is Everything

Jessica knew prom would be a hard sell. Her mother was already complaining about the tuition bill that was passed due and how the school always seemed to come up with extra things to pay for. Obviously, Jessica observed, this was not the moment to escalate her mom's venting by asking her to pay for prom. So, she waited. She waited for the right environment, place and timing. Jessica had learned by now that waiting until her mother had eaten dinner, soaked in the tub and settled down to watch television was the best move. Television time was really relaxed family time. Jessica could ask anything at that point.

Commercial breaks were perfect moments to chatter about prom. With nothing interesting to watch, Jessica's mom had now started giving her full attention to listening to the prom details. She had questions—lots of questions—and gripes, too. She listened to Jessica go on and on about grade improvements this year and she had excelled as the most valuable player on her volleyball team. Jessica didn't fail to mention what she was willing to do in exchange for her mother paying all her prom expenses: all the cleaning around the house, help her younger brother with homework each night and cook dinner twice a week until prom.

Jessica thought she had almost lost the bargain when she mentioned that she'd have more time to focus on her studies. But her mom just ignored that comment and reluctantly said, "Ok, Jess, but if you don't keep up with your end of the deal from now until a week before prom, the deal with be called off so fast you'll forget there even was a prom." She had to add that for the sake of preserving her authority. Jessica gave her mom a kiss and popped the family some popcorn.

The Breaking Point

Breaking through barriers like emotional and physical fatigue, can no doubt be challenging. However, as in Jessica's case, timing can make or break the sale. There will be some cases where you're just not as fortunate as Kristin or Tracy. Your parents or guardians may obstinately hold to a straight forward, "NO."

Here, and only here, is the time to transition into expressing a partial willingness to pay. Slowly unveil the things you are willing to pay for. Begin with exposing your willingness to pay for the least expensive thing. If that doesn't work, agree to pay for that and the next least expensive thing. Share these ideas one at a time and only if no agreement is reached.

Compromises:
1. Volunteer to pay for your nails if they pay the remainder
2. Assume responsibility to pay for your nails and accessories if they pay for the other expenses...

And so on until an agreement is made with them paying for something.

At An Impasse?

Throw yourself on the floor, roll around a bit. Then lock your arms around their legs and don't let go until they say they'll pay for everything. Ok, just kidding! Although you may have to cut your losses in negotiation with your parents or guardians, there is still hope.

Get Smart

Parents or guardians won't pay for your prom? No problem. Get someone else to pay for it! Even though parents or guardians may say they won't pay for your prom, they may agree to helping you raise the money for your prom.

Creative Ways to Raise Money for Prom:

1. Host a pre-prom party for an entry fee
2. Host a major garage sale or flea market where others can become vendors
3. Compose letters to family, friends and associates soliciting financial support

When All Else Fails

When there's absolutely no other way, you pay!

1. Save money received for allowances, birthdays, holidays and paychecks
2. Get a part-time job and save the money earned

Wait! That's Not All

Now that you know where your finances for the prom are coming from and you have chosen the right financial strategies for yourself, don't forget to create a prom budget.

I know, making a budget doesn't sound like fun, but in the end, you will be so happy you did! Preparing a budget says to those supporting you financially, "This girl's got it going on! She knows what she's doing!" It also says, "I can trust her with this money because she has already planned to stay within the amount I said I could give." A budget removes fear and doubt from those who are giving you money and it saves you from running out of money too soon.

Accessories	$
After Prom Activities	$
Boutonniere	$
Dress	$
Dress Alterations	$
Eyebrows	$
Hair	$
Hair Ornaments	$
Handbag	$
Hosiery	$
Make Up	$
Manicure	$
Pedicure	$
Photos	$
Prom Tickets	$
Shoes	$
Transportation	$
Total	$

Budgeting is easy: 1.) Know how much money is available to you; 2.) Know what items and services you will have to pay for and 3.) Plug in the numbers!

In addition to a budget, create a timeline so the person(s) paying for your prom will know how much money you'll need and when. A timeline that details the specific dates at which you'll need to purchase each item will make financial planning easier and less stressful. Happy bargaining!

My Prom Passion: Gathering My Resources

1. What information do I need to gather before trying to negotiate with my parents or guardians?

2. What financial resources are available to me?

3. What creative ideas can I turn into legal, money-making ideas?

4. How will I honor the generosity of my parents or guardians through the financial prom decisions I make?

5. What key purchases for prom can I absolutely not do without?

—*For Young Women Who Want More*—

Money forces us to choose. When it comes down to what we can purchase, the mighty dollar has much say. So, make things easier on yourself: use your resources. For girls who want more for their life, stealing is never an option, but there are some other ideas that can help you create the best night ever.

Is the fun you have at or after prom determined by how much money you have? No way! It's all about attitude and perspective. The person who spends the most on her dress isn't always the one who has the most fun—more often than not, she's the one most stressed trying to keep others from messing up her pricey threads. Those in the biggest, most loaded limos struggle to figure out how they're going to pay the bill. Moreover, those attending expensive or exclusive after-parties can experience more boredom than those who simply went around the corner. You don't need those headaches.

Your prom night will have as much energy, fun and excitement as you bring. Wherever you go can end up being the hottest place to be simply because of your expectations: expect to have a good time, to enjoy conversation and to make the most of where you are. *Your fun doesn't have to be tied to the amount of money you spend.*

Don't let lack of money get you down. You don't have to get caught up with spending a lot of money on prom just because others do. There's no shame in borrowing dresses, accessories or makeup from friends or family; in fact, it's a smart, money-saving idea! No one else will even know you borrowed them—just that you look absolutely great. So, focus your attention on what you do have, your creativity and people resources. **You can spend very little and still look your best!** Why spend lots of money when you don't have to?

-How much better to get wisdom than gold.-
-Proverb 16:16a-

Chapter 3

*I*magine *T*hat

Look around—they're everywhere! People and companies are searching for ways to influence your world. They want to influence what you wear, what you eat, where you'll go and with whom. There's no coincidence: they're after your identity.

Think about it. If red is the color of the season, other colors are hard to find. If pointy-toed shoes are hot, locating a square-toe will prove challenging. Moreover, the latest songs and music videos emphasize and promote certain thought patterns and values. Have you thought about the fact that advertisements cause you to long for things you never knew existed?

Is it true? How does it happen? Perhaps there's a meeting of the minds...

A Meeting of the Minds

Location—Anywhere
Time—Every ten years

Convener: Thank you, ladies and gentlemen, for attending this Summit. As you know, this is the time we meet at the exclusive *All About Us Retreat Center* to discuss how we can jointly impact what some call the "new generation." I hope you enjoyed our private jet service. As you read in the briefing packets sent to you ten years ago concerning our progress, failures and anticipated challenges, *All About Us, Inc.* has learned some significant information. Illusions, please turn off the lights. Let me draw your attention to our screen. Oh, yes, please relax and help yourself to the food, snacks and beverages provided—we are going to be here for quite awhile.

Here is a picture of Tiffany, Maria and Jasmine. These three teens, together, represent the "new generation." Let me point out to you that this "new generation" has several names: Millennium Generation, Generation Next and XGen. The Christians even have a term for them--The Solomon Generation.

For some of you new comers, it may seem ridiculous to meet on this beautiful mountain peak to talk about a bunch of bratty kids, but as you will soon learn, children grow into teenagers who have the capacity to turn the world upside down when given the proper information about who they are. And those same teenagers become adults who produce more children who can totally shut down this operation. Now, *All About Us, Inc.* doesn't intend to allow a bunch of high schoolers to put it out of business—

Everyone: "Here, here!"

Media Mouth: Convener, before we go any further, I would like to take thirty seconds to say that the media gives *All About Us, Inc.*, its full support, and has been committed to seeing its vision come to pass. Since the media's inception, particularly, radio, television, magazines and Internet, we have continued to shape the minds of children. And may I add that we have been completely successful in bombarding teens with so much access to information, they think everything is acceptable and everything must be tolerated. And furthermore-

Convener: Media Mouth, thank you for your expressions of loyalty. We must continue on, or we will truly be here for the next two years. Today we want to focus on teenagers—our Tiffanys, Marias and Jasmines. What is it that teenagers of this generation want?

Illusions: Freedom.

Death: Acceptance.

Illusions: Love?

Convener: Well, those are all great answers. I must say that Illusions said it best: love. Now the question is, 'Given what we know about the inner workings of the minds, emotions and character of this so-called Millennium Generation, how do we make these teen-agers do what we want, without them knowing we're taking away their freedom, twisting their sense of acceptance and giving them false love?'

Family Traits: By causing them to be worse than their parents. For instance, if their parents got hooked on alcohol, drugs or smoking, we can introduce these kids to it earlier and make it socially acceptable. If it's cool to drink with friends, do drugs after school or smoke in the bathroom, the teens will dive right in.

Illusions: I see your point, Family Traits.

Convener: This brings us to our strategy. That's what we're here for! History will now come and lead us in this next segment. We know it's important to understand our past so we can understand what's happening now and understand the right direction to choose for the future. History is our unbiased member—she gives us the facts and today, she will speak from our perspective. History...

History: Thank you, Convener. Yes, looking at past strategies will help us gain insight into how we need to raise up this "new generation." I'm not going to bore you with centuries of information—you know I have information from the very beginning of time. Today, I would like to focus on one particular seventh century BC king, Nebuchadnezzar, who was clearly on target when it comes to controlling a generation without it knowing. And after that brief synopsis, I will quickly move to the hot topic of the day: prom night.

Family Traits: I heard that Nebuchadnezzar had a whole generation of youth bowing in fear when certain music was played.

History: Family Traits, I see you've done your home-work. Yes, Nebuchadnezzar had one goal: to create a world that obeyed and served only him. Basically, he instituted a three pronged attack: Weaken young people's ability to distinguish between holy and unholy, remove young people's need to think for themselves and convince young people to accept a false identity.

Illusions: Brilliant!

History: He skillfully weaved everything together. Love was provided when the teens embraced a complete disdain for their God or an ambivalent atti-tude toward the God their people served. When the teens became disassociated with their own religion to follow whatever gods and spiritual experiences the king held dear, they received wonderful treat-ment—freedom and acceptance.

Media Mouth: Yes, we have done a few documen-taries on Nebuchadnezzar, hoping leaders across the

47

nations would embrace his strategies. As a matter of fact, Family Traits, by the time the king got done, he had completely brainwashed the youth and they didn't even know it. Just give me sixty seconds to tell you about it. Nebuchadnezzar took the young men from rich families and re-trained them for three years. They learned the king's language, the literature of his culture and were trained to serve him. It was kind of like being in the military—they did everything how and when the king commanded. They even ate certain food—only the best—so they would grow up strong. There were four boys who refused to bow to the music you were talking about earlier. Their names were Daniel, Shadrach, Meshach and Abednego. They almost ruined everything. They—

History: Media Mouth, we don't want to get into those troublemakers. But thank you so much for sharing. If you absolutely must know what these boys did, check out the first three chapters of the Book of Daniel in the Bible.

Convener: Thank you!

History: What Media Mouth pointed out was that King Nebuchadnezzar single-handedly shaped the minds of a generation. And so can we! Now the third area of attack was teen identity. It was absolutely imperative that the teens identified with the king and the king's culture. Anything less could have caused serious uprisings. By teaching the kids to identify with his culture, they only had his culture to look to in order to figure out who they were. So, when a Hebrew boy wanted to know how to be a Hebrew man, he didn't revert back to his Hebrew origin; he looked to the king's culture—the Babylonians.

Driving Under the Influence: Ok, so someone tell me what all of this has to do with the prom!

Convener: This year, our attacks will be aimed at female teens, D.U.I. Although the esteemed King Nebuchadnezzar only chose boys, we know from past experience that it's crucial to deal with girls, as well. These new young women are spunky. They are thinkers and we have to be very subtle if we are going to get anything by them.

Some of you have been very quiet—taking in all of this research, I'm sure. But now is the time for the rest of you to chime in. Let's get down to business.

D.U.I.: Alright, this is what I have been waiting for!

Illusions: My people have jumped right on this. Years ago we realized that in order to be ready for this meeting today, we had to set some things in motion. We have already launched Operation Acceptance. High School environments have been charged with gay, lesbian and bi-sexual confusion. It's becoming socially acceptable, now that more teens are open to trying these lifestyles. Some even believe they are one of the three, even though they aren't. Things are running pretty smoothly in that area. So, prom nights can be a little more exciting when we throw in teen girls desiring one another and satisfying each other sexually.

Convener: What about you, Death?

Media Mouth: If I could just say something before Death shares...We have already started pumping the airwaves, the television broadcasts, the malls, the magazines and the Internet with what we want teen girls to wear. Dress prices are sky high because we know every girl wants a dress no one else has. And we have stocked the stores with dresses that say, "If you want me, come get me!" You know what I mean? Slits up to the hip on both sides and large sections of the dress "missing." And we're telling the girls where all of the hot spots are for their after-prom activities—clubs, secluded parks, motels and the back seats of cars!

Convener: Media Mouth, please let Death speak.

Media Mouth: Excuse me for interjecting, Death. Go right ahead.

Death: My team has been working very diligently these last few years introducing new, more addicting and more lethal drugs on the market. LSD and Crack used to be our main drugs, but they were a little bold. This generation needs something a little less notice-able. So we have introduced GHB, which can be poured into the girls' drinks. The guys really get a kick out of this. They can do a train on the girls and they won't even know how many guys got on top of them while they were paralyzed and unconscious. We are also increasing the alcoholic beverages— minimizing the alcohol taste so the girls will indulge and not realize how much alcohol they've actually consumed. If we get the teen girls to drink with the boys, both will be drunk and deaths can increase— either their own deaths or the deaths of unexpected drivers and people walking on the streets.

Convener: Now, Media Mouth, what else would you like to add?

Media Mouth: I'm so glad you asked! I was just about to break in again. The one thing we have found to be effective from generation to generation is "slow jams." For those of you who don't know what "slow jams" are, they refer to slow music that sets an intimate and even sexual atmosphere. Teens in every generation swear by them and many girls lose their cool, dignity and virginity on prom night grinding to "slow jams" with their dates. The music just seems to take the teens to another place and they get lost in it.

Illusions: I know I haven't said anything in awhile. I must say that we have been working on breaking down the communication between this "new generation" and their parents. The breach seems to encourage a sense of false freedom and recklessness that teens just love. They feel invincible! We have also put fear of not being understood, fear of being misunderstood and fear of being "the only one" in youth's minds so they won't even try to talk to their parents' generation about prom night or anything else.

Convener: Well, it sounds like we are well underway. *All About Us* strives to—

Family Traits: Pardon me, Chairwoman. Are there any significant differences between the Tiffanys, Marias and Jasmines? They all seem to come from different cultures, backgrounds, economic situations, etc.

Illusions: No, Family Traits. That's the best thing about it. All of these girls want love and go after love. Whatever will make them "fit in" is what they are going to do. So we can have fun year after year, changing what's "in" and what's "out." We keep their heads spinning and their pockets empty. Soon enough, they will have to depend on one of us in this room. I have also made oral sex the new sex. Haven't you guys heard? Everyone's doing it! To avoid pregnancy and to "keep their man," girls have been persuaded that it's acceptable to put their mouths on guys' penises—oh, excuse me, I didn't mean to use that word. Anyhow, I have opened the door to sexual addiction and the girls don't even have a clue. Soon, their bodies will be so conditioned to being stimulated that they will have to constantly find ways to release that sexual tension and Death will have easier access than she has right now.

Death: My team has been having a field day! Nowadays, if teen girls don't have some kind of sexually transmitted disease, they are in the minority. I mean, about half of them will have some kind of STD before they leave high school. We are starting them younger and younger each year.

Illusions: I've been working on giving girls false love to the point some high schools have to recognize my work—they have daycare centers in the schools so teen mothers don't have to drop out. Prom night brings me many first time customers despite condoms, birth control pills, oral sex and "pulling out early." I'm probably the best at offering a complete, abrupt change of life for female teens. These teens aren't going to have a clue about their identity when we get finished! What a tragedy. To know where you came from, who you are and what you were born to do are things everyone needs to know in order to enjoy the fullness of life. It's a shame to think that this new generation is filled with such great potential, but it's not going to ever find out...

Death: Oh, Illusions, you are so sentimental and nostalgic! It's either us or them. Now, I'm giving my all to wipe these kids out before they realize they have power to combat every power we can use against them. If they ever figure that out, we are done! I'll get them all to kill themselves before they can decide to make wiser choices and actually find out why they were put on this earth in the first place.

Illusions: Did you all feel that shaking?

D.U.I.: Yeah, and we weren't driving under the influence, either.

Illusions: I'll look out the window to see if anyone has caught us together…As far as I can tell, the coast is clear, so let's continue.

History: I know that shaking. It's that shaking King Nebuchadnezzar felt whenever he thought of the power of those four boys' God. He created all children and He looks out for them. The problem is: He's everywhere. I'm sure He knows we are meeting here.

Family Traits: Of course He knows, but He allows us to meet and set things in motion because He has given this new generation, like every other generation, the ability to choose who and what will influence them: us or Him.

Death: I'm just glad they keep choosing us. I enjoy what I do!

Convener: Listen, I thank all of you, again, for your commitment to *All About Us*, Inc. We will come back together in ten years to evaluate our progress. Please take any of the remaining food and beverages—don't be shy! Remember, your private jets will leave here at the staggered time posted in your suites. This is just a precaution: we don't want anyone else to know that we have all joined together. And we definitely don't want anyone to find out about this corporation or our plans. Remember, loose lips sink private jets. Right, Death?

Death: That's right!

Back To Reality?

As fictitious as it sounds, the truth is all the characters in the story above seek to have influence in our lives. The media bombards us with messages it wants us to embrace. Illusions cause us to believe something is reality when it is only fantasy. History and family traits try to repeat our parents' mistakes in our lives. Magnetizing us to danger, driving under the influence of alcohol is hazardous to our future. As if that weren't enough, identity confusion pushes us into depression, strange thought patterns and destructive acts. Death then hovers around our life when we make choices without considering consequences.

Our reality is there will always be people and things that will try to steer us in some direction. Don't let others think for you! Make sure your eyes are open and your brain is thinking, so you don't find yourself living someone else's life or living a lifestyle someone else pressured you into.

My *Prom Passions*: *Questions* of I*nfluence*

1. What kinds of images and values am I bombarded with and how do they relate to my vision of prom?

2. Who or what is trying to influence the way I think?

3. Of all the influences (positive and negative) sending messages about prom night, whose advice have I embraced without question? Why?

4. What are some of the possible consequences of following the advice of influences unquestioningly?

5. What sources can I trust to tell me the whole truth and to seek my best interest?

—*For Young Women Who Want More*—

It takes courage to be unique—a pentagon in a circular world. Inside, we all want to be different, but tend to make choices that cause us to be like everyone else. Opinionated commentary, pressures to not stick out and our own desires to fit in rob us of being one of a kind. Unfortunately, many of us end up living a lie because we suppress our differences, quickly embrace accepted norms and give a false presentation of who we really are. This tendency lends itself to fear of rejection, which often becomes the invisible pair of scissors, removing our pentagon personality and smoothing out our edginess. Inevitably we find ourselves forced to be satisfied with blending in.

Become the trendsetter. Learn to think for yourself and dare to think outside the box. Consider, "Why am I doing this?" and "Where is this going to lead me?" To think outside the box is to not be limited to thinking like people around you. Your friends and classmates don't set the standards for your life; they aren't you and cannot live your life for you. *You were created to do great things—live like it!* At first, fear of rejection will try to keep you from tapping into your courage. Here's a hint: remember fear is like a little puppy with a big dog bark: it sounds intimidating, but it's really just a small thing you can master.

As a young woman of influence, you don't have to let fear keep you from knowing the truth. ***Don't settle for what others say—find out the truth, the whole truth and nothing but the truth for yourself.*** People tend to give us only enough information to lure us in, but won't warn us of what we're really getting into. They'll say things like "Just give him some head—you won't get pregnant." However, they won't tell you that although oral sex won't get you pregnant, it can leave you with external and internal signs of disease on your lips, in your mouth or in your body in general—temporary or permanent. That's why you want to know <u>*all*</u> the pros and cons before getting involved. Seeking out the whole truth may very well save your life, keep you from making bad decisions and protect you from danger. Kick fear to the curb and take courage: ***this is your life and you have control over your own decisions!***

-A [young woman] has great power, and a [young woman] of knowledge increases strength.-
Proverb 24:5

Chapter 4

Secret Journal

Courage refuses to allow her silence to rule one second longer. Listening anxiously to the other females chatter on about their after-prom plans for backseat escapades stirs a strong passion within her she didn't even know she had. She is searching for someone to tell her it's ok to not have sex, get drunk or compromise herself on prom night.

Who is this weird, young woman who dares to make decisions against the accepted norms of the junior high and high school soap operas? She is the popular girl and the girl no one seems to notice. She is a part of your inner circle of friends, the odd group of girls you don't understand and the clique with which you would never want to be associated. She is the athlete, the artist and the brainiac. Who is she? She could be you!

Her question finds its way into secret conversations, unplanned confessions, peer group discussions and even private prayers. The answer she is looking for is deep within her heart. Will she listen or will she settle for the answer her heart knows to be untrue?

In this chapter, I will share my answer with you. I now invite you to read my secret journal. Perhaps you'll discover your own thoughts, expectations and desires for your prom night.

A Heart's Betrayal

We had been together for a long time — a year and a half. We had talked about the possibility of having sex during the school year, but I told him I wasn't ready and I didn't want to get pregnant. He was good about honoring my request and I appreciated that he never pressured me.

It was Senior Prom and again I had to consider if we would have sex. I really liked him and I believed I loved him. I knew he cared about me and he said he loved me, too. He wasn't the kind of guy who had a list of girls he had slept with nor was he one to brag to his friends about what he had done with his girl. So I felt secure that our night together wouldn't become the topic of lunch conversation…but could I handle the consequences?

That night in the limo as we were whisked away to New York, he asked me again. I kept kissing him, hoping to distract him for a while. I had let him touch me just about everywhere, but the thought of allowing him to actually be inside of me went against what I believed and desired in my heart. I wanted more for myself and I knew I had a right to protect "me" and to have a standard for my life—and believe me, my standard was higher than most. After a long time of internal debate, I reasoned with myself, "I've made him wait long enough."

"I'm scared," I confessed, feeling the fullness of his weight on me. I was afraid of getting pregnant and afraid that having sex was going to hurt.

"Me, too," he whispered, searching for a sign of "yes" to surface in my eyes. After a few moments, I came to a decision. I decided to give in.

"Ok, we can."

"Are you sure?" I wasn't sure, but I prayed for God to have mercy on me.

"Yeah…"

Reality Check

The presence of his condom didn't take away my fears. I was still scared and I couldn't relax. Pinned to the plush leather seat, I wished I could sink into its blackness to find me in some other place, in some other moment in time. Attempting to not focus on all the things that could go wrong, I tried to distract myself from thinking about the condom breaking. Health Class was beating me in the head: *Condoms break and they won't protect me from every sexually transmitted disease…*

I tried not to think about what I would say to my parents if a month or two after that night I found myself pregnant. How could I even shape my mouth to verbalize *I* was *pregnant*? I could see the impending disappointment, hurt, disgust and embarrassment on my parents' faces. My father had done his best to get me through high school "with all my options open"—academically prepared for college with no children. I wasn't prepared to let him down.

My mother's side of the family was highly recognized in the community for its professional services. I had always heard about the importance of having a good reputation and always being aware of the fact that I represent the family. Shame and stigma were all I could imagine coming forth as a consequence.

While trying to enjoy the moment in the limo with the boyfriend I loved, my mind was bombarded with our conversation months earlier. He had expressed his preference for us to break up after graduation instead of staying together through college. I knew it would all be over in a few more weeks…How did I get here with him on top of me, inside of me?

When our moment of desire and passion was over, I had a feeling I didn't anticipate. I immediately thought, "I could have waited." Disappointment overflowed the floodgates of my heart and filled my mind. I wasn't disappointed in my boyfriend's sexual performance: I was disappointed in myself. I had wanted more for myself. My true desire and passion was to save myself for my husband, to be a virgin when I got married, to be a woman of excellence with true moral standards. In a matter of a few hours, for the sake of not ruining prom night for my boyfriend, I dropped every standard that was important to me. And it wasn't even worth it!

I thought I would be happy—I wasn't. For days and weeks to come, I prayed and searched. Every time I went to the bathroom, I would check, hoping to see some indisputable evidence proving I definitely wasn't pregnant. What would I say? What would I do? I was on an emotional roller coaster! I kept crying out to God for forgiveness. I kept telling God over and over again how sorry I was. It really hurt me; it hurt to know that I was not a virgin any more. It bothered me that if anyone asked if I had had sex before, I would have to say yes—I wanted to be able to say no.

I had put my life in jeopardy. In one moment I could have destroyed any chance of going to college. I had worked diligently to have and maintain high grades so I could get scholarships to go to college for free. All of that hard work could have gone down the drain. It never occurred to me to get tested for STDs—as far as I knew, he didn't have anything, but you can't always tell and people aren't always honest. I could've had to deal with the realities of being a teenaged mother raising her child alone. What was I thinking?

It seemed like eternity…How soon would I know if I were pregnant or not? The wait was almost unbearable. Finally, one day as I did my usually check, I saw my period had come and believe me, I was relieved! I was relieved and most of all thankful that God did not allow my life to take that fateful turn.

Betrayed Twice

As grateful as I was, I still had to face the reality of betrayal. The betrayal I experienced on prom night was not only against my heart, but also against my body. At the beginning I was determined to honor my body. I refused to allow any boy to devalue my body by turning it into a sex object or a thing to be bought with convincing guilt trips or "I loves yous." My initial conviction to not have sex was my meager attempt to protect and recognize of the value of my body—although I had already disrespected myself by allowing my body to be subjected to inappropriate touches. However, I ended up completely dishonoring my body when I allowed it to be exposed to the dangers of disease, the traps of increasing appetite for sexual experiences and the possibility of pregnancy before marriage. True honor could have been displayed through a simple "No, we aren't having sex or messing around on prom night."

I know honoring requires courage because it takes boldness to hold on to what your heart considers valuable when others continually deem it worthless. Regardless of the struggles, honoring your body will bring you peace and joy, knowing that you are being true to yourself.

A Right to Be True To Yourself

Being true to yourself is worth the internal wrestling because your body is a precious gift. You only get one body: although it can be cosmetically altered,

you can't exchange it or get a new one. Its preciousness calls for special attention and careful consider-
ation, so learn to honor your body!

Your body gives you power, which can be positive or negative. Your body is not an object to be
used to secure affection, attention or relationship.
Your body is not even the totality of who you are:
you are more than your physical body! Whether you
wear bikinis, sweat suits, overalls or prom dresses,
your body captures attention—particularly from
males. That ability to suggest, persuade and influence requires that you learn to honor your body or
else you will abuse it.

Did you know others will treat your body the
way you treat it? Honoring your body doesn't mean
throwing a party to celebrate its preciousness or hiding
it under layers of clothing to keep it from being seen.
To honor doesn't even mean to set it on display by
exposing it to the world. Honoring your body means
you highly regard, recognize and respect it.

To regard your body highly is to acknowledge its
value and worth. If the body you have is the only one
you will have in this life, it's priceless! We take care
of things we value and we protect them from unnecessary abuse and damage. Choosing to not have sex or
sexual explorations on prom night (or any other night)
is one way of expressing true honor to your body.

Recognizing your body's worth includes acknowl-
edging its needs and desires. Your body needs regular
exercise, healthy eating habits and rest. Your body
also has desires—some constructive and others
destructive. You must determine which desires to

pursue and which desires to deny for the well-being of your body.

Respecting yourself means making daily choices that protect your physical body from abuse, violation and devaluation. In essence, to be true to yourself, you must make decisions that show how much you appreciate the physical body you have been given.

No Disrespect

Don't be fooled! You deserve respect and you should demand it. However, it's guaranteed you'll experience disrespect if you don't set a standard and express how you want to be treated.

We all have ways of determining what we will or won't do. Some of us compare ourselves with others—what they have done, want to do or would never do. Others of us choose our actions by how we feel, what we see on music videos, what we hear on the radio or what we're told in church.

The standards we hold for our lives say a lot about how we view ourselves. Standards establish boundaries that clearly distinguish between "this is me" and "this is not me." Low standards can be identified by the ease of compromise at the slightest request. High standards, on the other hand, show you have a pretty clear understanding of who you are; you are determined to be respected by others and you take seriously the goals and dreams you aspire to achieve.

Maintaining the standards you have for your life is not anyone else's responsibility except your own. If standards are to be kept, you have to be willing to stand up for who you are, demand respect for yourself and not allow your value to be cheapened. Others will test you to find out what your standards are—whether they are real or fake. Believe me, people will go as far as you allow them!

Where Does Disrespect Begin?

Kissing: On the hand? the forehead? the neck?
the ear? the breast?
the center of your thighs?

Touches: On uncovered skin? the face? the arm? the waist? the behind? under the skirt?
inside the underwear?

Sexual Experimentation: Mere suggestion?
oral sex? masturbation?
sexual intercourse?

Remember, you are the most valuable thing you have! What you allow or give into sends a clear message to yourself and others about who and what you are.

Respect 101

Reflecting back on my night in the limo, the decisions I made to say "yes" taught my boyfriend there was room for exploration. It started with a "yes" to his hands on my chest and behind long before prom night. Once his hands got used to being in those places, they wanted access to other parts of my body. I then moved to a "yes" to hands under my shirt, and the "yeses" continued to give more access to disrespect. This progression continued until having sex became a natural inquiry and a possible option. Those "yeses" were not representative of who I was or who I wanted to be. Each "yes" attempted to chip away at my hopes, dreams and aspirations, for I became compromised. I started to accept less than what I was due. I was due respect, honor and appreciation. It seems I gave myself away for cheap even though I was more valuable than a flawless diamond!

The Diva Queen

Have you heard about Queen Vashti? She remained true to her heart by honoring her body more than her desire for male attention and power. Now, you might say, "That's probably because she was ugly and no one wanted her anyway!" But read what was said about Vashti:

[The King commanded his servants] to bring before him
Queen Vashti, wearing her royal crown, in order to display her beauty to the people and nobles, for she was lovely to look at. But when the attendants delivered the king's command, Queen Vashti refused to come. Then the king became furious and burned with anger.
−Esther 1:11-12−

Vashti was neither ugly nor stupid. In fact, the king only chose the most beautiful woman among all women of the land to be queen. Queen Vashti refused to be a showpiece! She was not going to parade her body in front of men whose minds were heavily influenced by drunkenness. She didn't let her body be displayed before these men, to be touched or inappropriately fantasized about in their minds. The beauty of her physical body was to be reserved for her husband's full attention alone: she did not set foot in that room. When you know who you are and the things of value you possess, you don't try to prove anything: Vashti was beautiful and she knew it! The queen did not allow her body to be dishonored for the sake of feeding her man's ego or to make herself look more desirable to other men on that special night. Why should you?

What Will You Remember?

Like Nikki, Aaliyah and Sarah from our first chapter, you probably have some ideas about what you want to experience on your prom night. Expectations are more likely to come true when you think things all the way through and make decisions in line with those expectations. Have you really thought about why you want those experiences or what kind of memories those experiences might bring you? Here are some questions to help make your dreams come true:

My *Prom Passions*: *Questions That Matter*

1. What is my heart's true desire as it relates to the prom?

2. How will my future life, dreams and aspirations be affected if my sexual experiences don't go as planned?

3. What standards do I need to set for my own life so others don't disrespect or degrade me?

4. How will I respond if my date persists even after I've clearly said "No"?

5. To keep myself from being physically and emotionally betrayed, to what must I courageously say "No"?

—*For Young Women Who Want More*—

Make decisions for tomorrow—not just today. In the heat of the moment, it's easy to get involved in things simply because "the feeling is so right." However, feelings that seem so right are often so wrong for us. It can feel so right to say "Yes" to a boy's every physical desire, but the end result could be a loss of respect, public humiliation, the stigma of a reputation for being "easy", etc. Remember to consider the rest of your life—your aspirations, goals and the desires of your heart. These things are more important than one night.

If you haven't had sex already, you don't want to lose your virginity on Prom night—there's too much at stake. Having sex exposes you to possibilities of infection, a guilty conscience, rejection from your date and low self-esteem. "Messing around" doesn't even need to be an option because you don't have to compromise. *It may seem like everyone else is doing it, but there are so many who wish they never had.* Express respect for yourself by refusing to jeopardize your future.

"What if I've already had sex before?" you ask. It's never too late to start over, to decide from this day forward your physical body is off limits to intimate touches until marriage. Sexual explorations don't make you more of a woman. A woman takes the responsibility to make decisions for herself mainly based on principal and dignity--not mere feelings because feelings are often unpredictable and irrational. *Think about this: When the boy is gone, what will he have left you?* Disease, a baby, self-hatred or shattered self-image? Express respect for yourself by refusing to jeopardize your future any longer.

We can't take back our actions. Once we sow our actions, we are bound to reap consequences and we never know how much we'll have to face. Each time we make a decision that is less than safe, we wonder if we are going to "get away with it," if we'll have to deal with one minor repercussion or if we'll have to experience an avalanche of an ordeal. *Since you are ultimately responsible for what happens in your body, don't let another person compromise its purity or undermine its worth.*

-Say to wisdom, "You are my sister."-
Proverb 7:4a

Chapter 5

My W*orld*

Everyone was talking about it. Vibrating cell phones prompted girls to get excused from class to hear details about the atrocity. The information superhighway was ablaze during Free Period with students emailing heated responses about what happened. Huddles of girls formed around hall lockers between classes to express outrage. Other girls fearfully clutched their boyfriend's arm as they walked down the hallways, promising to fulfill threats if they dare look at another female. Juicy rumors buzzed in everyone's ears that morning announcing that Mercedes had struck again: another male upper classman had fallen into her trap.

"What? Can I help it if I'm in high demand?" Mercedes' name was all over school. Her reputation and popularity had been increasing steadily since 7th grade. Most boys were crazy about her; almost all the girls hated her.

Since smelly cafeteria food left much to be desired, even Friday pizza couldn't hinder the windstorm of unstoppable conversation. Lunch Period proved to be like all the others that day—Mercedes and Gorge were the main topic of discussion.

"C'mon, Mere', what was he like?" Drooling pizza grease, Juana was anxious to find out about Gorge. Gorge was a serious jock with irresistible dark brown curls and the sexiest green eyes imaginable. Every girl dreamed of capturing his attention.

"I've heard he's a jerk. If so, he sure is a really HOT jerk!" Cynthia chimed in, slapping hands mid air with Maria. "I heard some other girls talking about him in the locker room after gym last week. They said he's a real dog. What do they expect? He can have any girl he wants."

"Wait a minute! Are you trying to call me easy? They may say that Gorge can have any girl he wants, but he can't have me!" Mercedes felt a need to defend herself among her friends.

"You're just like the rest of them, Amiga. You already said he had you, remember?" Juana quickly recalled Mercedes' boastful musings of irresistibility. Licking her fingers, Juana had to admit that she was eating some good pizza; well, anything beats the mystery meat served in the cafeteria on Thursdays.

"No. I didn't say he had me. I said *I* had him," Mercedes insisted.

"What do you mean? You both had each other at the same time." This conversation was all too complicated for Maria, as she tried to finish her math equations before the period was over. She liked to keep things simple—only boyfriends could get physical with her. Maria found it difficult to understand how Mercedes could so easily mess with different boys at one time and none of them seemed to care.

"Let me break it down for you. No one can be with me unless *I* say so. If they want to be in *my* world, they have to go by *my* rules" Mercedes asserted. "If a boy wants to come into Mercedes' world, he *has* to respect me to the utmost. What *I* say goes…"

"Yeah, and thank God *anything* goes in your world, girl!" Jimmy rejoiced, licking Mercedes' ear as he strolled pass the girls' table on his way to the Guidance office. Beaming from ear to ear at the remembrance, Jimmy's mind went back to that day he and Mercedes had sex in the woods right behind the school before getting picked up after track practice.

"Shut up, Jimmy! Nobody was talking to you! Get out of here!" the girls shouted, shoving Jimmy away and quickly returning to their fascination with Mercedes' world.

"Like I was saying, what I say goes. I have standards—if the guy doesn't respect me, then he's not worth my time."

"Mere, I hate to say it, but what Jimmy said really is true. In your world, anything goes. But me…a boy can't even rub all over my body unless we've been together for a month" Maria had to say as she erased her wrong answer to a word problem.

"R.E.S.P.E.C.T. That's what I want and that's what I demand!" Mercedes reiterated. "Not everyone can get with me. Anyone who meets me at the mall can't push up on me and expect to get my number. I don't mess with anyone who has dated or messed with any of you—"

"Ok, wait a minute. Do you remember last year when you told us how you had spent a night with Jose? Jose and I were messing around one year before that!" Cynthia didn't want her to forget.

"Alright, but that was different. I was hanging out with some of my peoples from New York. Everyone else was paired off and the two of us didn't have anything to do, so we found our own spot and started messing around, too. That doesn't count, Cynth."

"Mere, you know that really hurt me. Jose and I were kind of talking then..." Cynthia's comment was quickly blown off.

"Forget about it! That doesn't count, Cynth" Mercedes insisted. "Like I was saying, I am a queen. You have to have standards, girls. The guys I mess with have to take me out, and I don't mean to Mc Donald's or some rinky dink place. They have to buy me presents and do what I want. And let me tell you--not everyone can pay the price. You know what I mean? I'm a diva! What can I say?"

"I don't know if that's respect, though. If you respected yourself, I would think you wouldn't have sex with all these guys. You wouldn't be out there trying to build a reputation for sleeping with other people's men or treating them like trash," Maria asserted.

The conversation had obviously gone to the next level, but Maria didn't care. Deciding she'd settle for an incomplete on the math homework next period,

Maria took Mercedes' diva comments personal. She didn't care that their voices had escalated, that the teachers on lunch duty could hear them or that her emotions were sprawled all over the table. Mercedes needed to learn that everything wasn't about her.

"Maria, what is your problem?" Mercedes snapped back. "You're just mad Jonathan hasn't asked you to be his girl even though you've been going down on him since last month. Don't be a hater because you don't know what to do with your man to make him stay." Those were fighting words and Mercedes' was testing Maria to see if she was up for the challenge.

Attempting to change the subject upon seeing Maria's eyes turn fiery red, Juana jumped in. "So, diva, we haven't talked about prom yet. Who'll get to be in Mercedes' World that night? What about Charles? He's been sweatin' you since the beginning of the school year. Or...wait a minute...what about *Stevie Nicks*?!"

"I haven't decided. I have needs, you know? Charles is a sloppy kisser, but Stevie...Stevie knows how to make a girl feel good. Last summer we got into some things at his house when his parents were out of town one weekend. Every room—but our time in his parents' bed was the sexiest."

"What?! Girl, you are crazy!" Natalia busted out, throwing her head all the way back in sheer laughter. She had been silent until now, but the girls had learned that Natalia didn't miss much. Food captured Natalia's attention, but she was always listening. So the girls were used to talking among themselves at meal times until Natalia emerged from the depths of her plate.

"I didn't tell you?"

"No! You left that one out. Mercedes' World is definitely exciting, but I just don't see how you do it, girl. It's a wonder we haven't had to take you to the clinic over the last few months." Natalia was a straight shooter. That's why Mercedes loved and hated to have her around. The girls at the table always wondered why Natalia liked them—she was so extremely different than all of them when it came to boys.

"I can't worry about that...I know what I'm doing and I can handle it. I'm not afraid to get pregnant and I'm not scared of some disease. I like to have sex and I like to have it with a lot of people. What's wrong with that? I figure, if I or the guys catch anything, we have it coming to us anyway. Whatever happens, I'll just deal with it."

"I used to think that way, too, until I realized that having sex wasn't changing anything. Every time, I was trying to use sex to help me deal with my pain, but having sex wasn't going to bring my dad back home or make me feel better about myself—it made me feel worse." The girls were used to hearing this kind of stuff from Natalia. Most of the time they tolerated it, but they had to admit to themselves that sometimes what she said really made sense.

"Well, Oh Sainted One, who are you going to the prom with?" Juana inquired of Natalia. Admittedly, Natalia had really changed over the years. After attending a family psychologist because her mother didn't know what else to do with her, Natalia had really become level headed.

"You know who I'm going with. Bobby, of course." The likes of Mercedes couldn't stand to be in relationship with the likes of Bobby. Bobby was amazing. He knew how to make a girl feel special and appreciated. The thought of being with someone like Bobby was repulsive to Mercedes, who really didn't know how to be in a relationship without giving her body.

"Of course!" Mercedes mockingly imitated.

"Yeah, Bobby asked me to the prom last week. We already started talking about it."

Maria wanted to rub some more alcohol into Mercedes' wounds. She knew how Mercedes really felt: Mercedes didn't care about herself. Everyone in the group knew that ever since her uncle raped her when she was in 7th grade, Mercedes had never been the same. Everyone knew that she had sex with all these guys because she really hated herself and her body.

"So you guys aren't going to get a little taste of each other on prom night? Don't you think you owe it to yourself, Natalia? You've been such a good girl and you and Bobby have been boyfriend and girl-friend for two years already. Even I'm planning on letting some things slide on prom night." Maria confessed.

"There won't be any tasting that night or any other night. Y'all don't think I'm serious. I keep telling you that nothing is happening up in here. I love myself too much to let some guy touch all over my body and be all in it with no real commitment to me. You guys were talking about respect before, and when it comes to that, I know that I'm worthy of respect, that I have learned to respect myself and require others to respect me."

"Aw, here we go with that psychology stuff again." Mercedes grumbled as she sunk her teeth into a cold slice of pepperoni pizza. "Isn't the bell about to ring?"

Throwing the slice back on its greasy plate, Mercedes got up from the table and walked over toward the candy stand to get a closer look at the clock and to get away from Natalia's voice. Mercedes always started to feel bad when Natalia started to talk about things she had learned through the psychologist. *What if what Natalia said was true?* she thought as she wiped the pizza grease on a napkin pulled from an overstuffed canister at the counter. Well, maybe if Mercedes didn't hear what Natalia said, disappointment, anger and fear wouldn't creep back into her heart.

Returning to the table, Mercedes was ready to have all the attention again. "Well, girls, I think I've decided. I'm going to let Gorge take me to prom. "

"Yeah, I was trying to tell you before," Cynthia remembered, "that last week the girls in my gym class were whispering about how Gorge had slept with Judy—you know she goes with Carlos. They said Judy was all tore up about it because he started calling her all kind of names while they were messing around and when she wanted him to stop, he got right on top of her until he was finished." Cynthia didn't feel one way or another about it. She just wanted Mercedes to know.

To be honest, that locker room conversation had made Juana rethink why she always ended up naked, hiding in some guy's basement or worrying about disease, when her parents were doctors. They always told her, "You only get one body, so take care of it the best you can." The phrase had become an increasingly annoying thought as Lunch Period moved along.

"I heard some guys talking about it when I was on the way to English. They were telling Gorge to be careful because Judy's parents had come up to the school. But before the bell rang, I heard Gorge say he was going to "get his" and he didn't care about Judy or any other girl here." Maria shared, now recalling the incident more clearly.

"That's exactly what I'm talking about." Natalia reiterated. "You have to make a guy respect you. Judy chose to get involved with a guy who has a reputation for going through girls like underwear. All the signs were telling her to not get involved with him at all. Now she's had sex with him and may have been raped. And for what?"

"For a good time!" Mercedes chimed in.

Juana had been pretty quiet for a while. She couldn't help thinking about her own prom night and who her date would be and what they might or might not do. Juana really identified with what Natalia said about respect. Guys felt like they could say anything and do anything to Mercedes—didn't she see that? Respect, in Juana's mind, had to be something else. Obviously, giving her body didn't make any boy stay and giving a boy what he kept asking for didn't make her feel good about herself. Wasn't it almost time for lunch to be over? Juana was feeling uneasy, like she had a decision to make.

Ring! Finally, lunch was over. Maria snatched up her book bag and stuffed her Math book between some notebooks. Mercedes took three huge bites of what was left of her cold, pepperoni pizza. Natalia threw everyone's plates in the garbage next to the table and Cynthia refreshed her make-up, knowing Jose would be in her next class.

But Juana—she just sat there with tears welling up in her eyes. She tried to hide it by pretending to put something in her book bag, but she hadn't taken anything out of it. Mercedes noticed that some wet drops were falling on the seat beneath Juana's head. Wiping the pizza sauce from her mouth, Mercedes put her hand on Juana's back, "Hey girly. Are you alright?"

"I…I…This is too much." Juana managed to force herself to say.

"What do you mean, Juana?" Cynthia asked, looking over her hand mirror.

"This is just too much." Juana sniffled. "Prom's coming up and all of us, except Natalia, don't know who we're going with." Blowing her nose on a tissue that appeared out of nowhere, Juana continued, "All we know is that someone's going to have to pay. Mercedes tries to hide behind sex. Maria, even though she really didn't want to, is now willing to risk getting herpes blisters on her mouth just to get Jonathan to take enough interest in her to ask her out to the prom. Cynthia has been having sex with Jose to make him forget about Mercedes. And I don't know what respect is anymore."

Breaking down uncontrollably, Juana just wanted to run out of school. The girls huddled around her to shield her from being seen by the teacher on duty and the other kids walking by.

Natalia didn't know what to say. All she could think to do was say what came to mind. So she took a tissue and helped Juana wipe the tears away. Then some words popped into her mind.

"Hey, Juana. It's ok to cry—I know I cried when it seemed like I didn't know who I was or what I wanted anymore. I cried because I was afraid and because I wasn't sure what to do or what to feel. I didn't even know who to believe or who to trust. But the tears stopped and the confusion stopped when I started to become honest with myself.

"What do you mean?" Juana whispered.

"I mean that the tears stopped after I made some tough decisions. I had to decide what was best for me. I had to start living what I knew was true. Juana, you know what's true. You know how your parents are always saying, "You only get one body, take care of it the best you can?"

"Yeah." Natalia took her by the hand and helped her to stand up. She picked up Juana's book bag and put it on her shoulder as they turned and started heading toward the cafeteria doors.

"It's true. Yeah, we only have one body, but we are also more than just our body. You're body is a part of you, just like your mind, your emotions, your heart and your personality are a part of you. I decided that all of me was going to work together. So, I don't have to have sex, do what I'm uncomfortable doing or endanger my life. I love me and I respect me. You can have that, too, but you have to make that decision for yourself."

Natalia didn't know if what she said made sense and Juana didn't know what choice she'd make. However, everyone in the group knew they had to make some new decisions—before prom night even came around. Those decisions would reshape their worlds and although they weren't sure what those worlds would look like, they were sure of one thing: everyone, including themselves, would have to respect it.

Making the Decisions

Can you really create a new and different world for yourself? Of course! One major power each of us possesses is the ability to choose. Just like we choose what style of clothing we wear, the friends we hang with and the attitudes we have, we also reserve the right to change the way we think about things. You might say, "Change is hard." It is, but changing for the better is worth every bit of effort it takes. So start with small changes and be consistent with them. Sooner than later, those small changes will become a part of who you are. Others will be uncomfortable with your changes at first, but if you stay focused on your re-creation, they'll have to accept it as your new reality. Don't settle for less. Make a conscious decision to face and conquer the fear of change and rejection. You'll be glad you did!

My *Prom Passions*: Reshaping Your World

1. Am I who I really want to be?

2. If having a date for prom is an option, what kind of person would I like to take to the prom?

3. What people or experiences have shaped my attitudes about sex and the value of my body?

—*For Young Women Who Want More*—

CAUTION! CONSTRUCTION SITE: HARD HATS A MUST. Re-creating your world is no easy task, but very rewarding and beneficial. As with any construction project, the question "How do I really want this to be?" must be answered. Start with a vision, an idea of what you want your world to be — regardless of what your world is like right now. Then, with that vision in mind, lay out a plan of action, considering each major and then minor thing that must be done to create what you've imagined. Using all necessary resources, begin construction: knock down and clear out all presence of the old, lay a new solid foundation and build with appropriate materials.

Being under construction is an exciting time because the possibility of what can be is the motivation for action — no matter how tedious, strenuous or dangerous the re-creating might be. The work of constructing is worth the effort to create a better, meaningful and emotionally healthy world. Aaaah... *Imagine that — loving life, being free of emotional heaviness and adding something of value to the lives of everyone who comes into contact with you.*

Construct your world with the BEST MATERIALS ONLY. Let the foundation of your world be an extremely positive view of who you are. Seeing yourself as beautiful, accepted, priceless and loved "as is" will shift every decision and action you make. A positive view of yourself can keep you from allowing yourself to be taken advantage of, being disrespected, doing things that are killing you on the inside, hiding in the background or allowing everyone else to define you. As you build, don't forget to construct the walls of your world with your right to be protected and secure. Other quality materials include your faith, fullness of truth, joy and uncon- ditional self-love. *You have a right to give yourself the best chance to live an enjoyable, quality life, no matter what your past was like.*

Some life materials are reserved for the garbage because they attract flies and other annoying things that will hover over your life. These rotten materials are such things as hurt, pain, hopelessness, unnecessary drama, depression and emotions that weigh you down. If you build your world with these toxic materials, your new world will be the constant source of abuse, pain for yourself and others, limitations, disappointment and slow death. *So, refuse to build your world with negative images of yourself, half-truths and thinking that leads to your destruction.*

You are one of the great wonders of the world, worthy of admiration for the quality choices you make to acquire and maintain your inner character and outer poise.

-She watches over the affairs of her household.-
Proverb 31:27a

Chapter 6

Me, My Date and Who?

─◁◎〰▷─

Last minute purchases and primping make prom day one of the craziest. There never seems to be enough time! Even if things manage to go smoothly during the day, the ride to the prom can prove more interesting than anticipated. You never know whom you'll meet or all you'll have to go through just to get to there...

"My mom is trippin' again. I still have to make dinner for my little brother and make sure he's ready for my dad—you know this is his weekend with us. I'm SO glad prom is tonight! I need to dance the night away and the limo is picking me up in less than three hours." Sasha hurriedly rummaged through the refrigerator, searching for left-overs.

"It's so exciting. Wait, did I tell you about my crazy trip to the tattoo place?" Sasha's friend, Kierra, always had a dramatic story to tell.

"Kierra, I really have to go. My cell is about to die and I need to make sure it's charged up in case Jason or my dad calls."

"Alright, Sash. Call me when you get in the limo!"

"Ok." Sasha knew good and well she wasn't going to call Kierra from the limo. Just as Sasha scooted her brother out the door and skillfully avoided having to hug her father, the phone rang. It was Jason.

"Hey, Baby. It's me."

"What's up?"

"The limo company just called. I don't know what their problem is, but they said after checking our order, they decided to give us a larger limo at the same price."

"Cool! Now we'll have more space to get our freak on!" As soon as she got in that limo, all of her issues would melt away when Jason pulled her close.

"Yeah, Babe. And I can't wait to see you in that sexy dress." Jason was already bulging at the thought. Sasha was *fine* and any man would want to get with her. He still couldn't figure out why she wanted to have sex all the time, but he wasn't complaining. In attempts to keep up with Sasha all year, he had started surfing online to learn some new moves. "I've been working out all week. I'm going to make you holla', Baby."

"What time will the limo be here? Did you ask about the one with the spinning rims?"

"The limo has the rims and it should be there at... let me grab the paper. Hold up." As Jason searched for the invoice, Sasha leaped across the room and peeped out her third floor window covered by a thick film of accumulated dust. Mom never checked to see if she had actually cleaned the windows in her room.

"They said five o'clock."

"Five o'clock?! Why do we have to leave an hour and a half before we even have to be there? Oh, they're crazy!" Sasha couldn't imagine being ready that soon.

"Chill, Baby…That just means we have more time alone. Now that's what *I'm* talking about!"

"Alright, Jay, I really have to hurry now. Let me go—and don't forget your top hat."

"Peace."

Sasha made a mad dash for the bathroom. Five o'clock? That was in an hour! Maybe someone waved a magic wand or maybe God really did hear her when she asked for help. Whatever happened, she was ready at 4:50pm on the dot. Despite the rush, she looked fabulous. She wished she could look like that every day—classy and sophisticated. She looked like a princess from a fairy tale.

People in the neighborhood started milling around outside as if some radio station van was riding through town giving out free stuff. What were they all looking at?

The moment she stepped onto her porch, she saw a huge monstrosity of a vehicle turn the corner. What was it? It was like a two level limo. But it was sleek. Then she saw them. The rims were spinning and she knew that vehicle had come to pick her up.

"You've got to be kidding!" Sasha blurted out. The driver stopped right in front of her steps, opened her limo door and said, "Miss Sasha, I presume?"

"Yes." Sasha scrunched up her face, wanting to avoid being embarrassed.

"Please step in, Princess. We have a long journey." What did he mean by "a long journey?" The Manor was fifteen minutes from Jason's and Jason lived seven minutes from her house—she had timed it.

I can't wait to see Jason, Sasha thought dreamily as the vehicle luxuriously floated down the street. Even though she had been using him to get what she wanted all year, she realized that Jason really liked her. Yes, they did have sex pretty regularly, but he took time to find out what she thought and what she wanted to do in her life. He really cared about her. Somehow Jason had made her see that although sex felt good, there was more to life. Somehow, he made her believe she could do more and be more.

In seven minutes, the "limo" was parked in front of Jason's house. He looked so good in his tux! As soon as Sasha stepped out the limo, cameras started flashing from everywhere. It was like being a star walking down the Hollywood red carpet—into a family reunion. Jason's whole family was there. Cousin T was hanging out the second-floor window, filming with the video camera. Aunt Charletta was standing at the bottom of the steps. Jason's mom was snapping digital pictures from the porch and his dad was snapping a *Fun Saver* from the bathroom window. Sasha felt like this day was all about fulfilling her fantasies. And she definitely wanted to be a star!

When she came back to herself and stopped the beauty queen wave, Jason was standing in the door way. He floated down the steps like a fine brotha' in the movies. The top hat and the cane set it off.

"……..Man, girl. Let's get in this…What is it?" he asked, wiping his mouth to remove her Luscious Berry lip gloss from his lips. Eyes wild with amazement, Jason threw the cane down and started jumping.

"Yo, I don't know what this is, but it's fire!" The double-leveled limo was a guy's dream come true.

"Excuse me, Master Jason. We must be leaving; we have a long journey ahead of us."

"What do you mean, Dog? The Manor is fifteen minutes from the crib" he said as the driver shut them both in the limo. "What is he talking about, Baby?"

"I don't know. He said that to me, too. Do you think he got us mixed up with kids from another school?" Sasha wondered.

"Who knows? Well, let the games begin!"

"Hey! No cheating!" Sasha screamed. Jason's shirt wasn't even buttoned under his jacket—it was Velcro! As soon as Sasha started to unzip herself, the limo stopped.

"What the…" They both peeked out, fogging the window with their hot breath. Where were they? They were only around the corner, but they were on "the other side of town." Before they knew it, the limo driver was ringing someone's doorbell. The door opened, but their eyes couldn't peer around the corner to see who answered. The driver came back, opened the limo door and escorted them into the mystery person's living room.

"Miss Teach will be with us momentarily. She just finished grading the essays you both turned in the other day. She said you are welcome to take a look around."

"Why are we at Miss Teach's house, Man? We've got a prom to get to."

"Is this some kind of sick joke? Taking us to Miss Teach's to get our essay grades right before prom? Jay, what's going on?"

"I really don't know, Boo," he said, discretely zipping the back of her dress. Miss Teach had jazz playing…it was pretty cool. From the family pictures on the mantle, they saw she was married, had children and played basketball in a women's league.

"Surprised?" Miss Teach entered the living room while they whispered about her life outside of school. "You didn't think you'd be going to the prom alone, did you? After all the things I've taught you this year in Health class, you better believe I would be here for your big day to make sure you guys are protected."

"You're coming with us?" Sasha and Jason said in chorus.

"Yes, she is. May we all return to the vehicle? We have a long journey ahead of us."

The driver assisted Miss Teach with her shawl and opened her front door.

"Is someone else coming also?" Miss Teach inquired. "Lovely!"

Back to the limo they all went—Sasha, Jason, Miss Teach and the driver. There was an awkward silence to say the least. Sasha kept thinking about her grade on the essay. Jason, on the other hand, kept wondering what kind of underwear Sasha was wearing. Noticing their discomfort, Miss Teach reached into the fridge and three minutes later said, "Pina Colada, anyone?"

The limo pulled over again, this time parking in front of a church. The driver opened the limo door and escorted them inside. As they walked toward the front of the sanctuary, Miss Teach expounded on the history of the architecture. Right at a key point in her lecture, the group found themselves knocking on the pastor's office door.

"Hello! I was just wrapping up my sermon for Sunday morning. I have been in great anticipation of this night. This will be a very special night, and I am so honored to share it with both of you."

Sasha knew it might be rude, but she leaned over to Jason and in a whisper that was rather loud said, "What is Rev. Faith talking about? Who said he could go with us to the prom? Step into my office *please!*" Standing behind the sanctuary pillar, they began to go back and forth.

"Jay, what does Rev. Faith have to do with our prom? I'm not trying to think about God, what I believe, the Bible or anything else religious. I just want to have a good time in the limo, to have fun dancing and to make love to you tonight."

"Baby, I really don't know what's going on."

"Tell him he can't go to the prom with us," Sasha insisted.

"*You* tell him he can't come with us! I can't tell God not to come."

"Jay, he's not God! He's Rev. Faith, our school chaplain!"

"Well, I'm ready! Let me just fix my clergy collar, here. You know what? Why don't we just head to the limo and I will adjust my collar as we walk out the door?" Fidgeting with the office key, Rev. Faith smiled cheerfully.

"Sounds splendid, Rev. Faith. We do have a long journey ahead of us." *A long journey ahead of us* echoed in Sasha's ears like a repeated line in a horror movie.

"Huuuh!" Flustered and edgy, Sasha reappeared from behind the column, snatched Jason's hand, rolled her eyes, sucked her teeth and stomped her way out of the church—all in one motion.

After quickly locking the church doors and positioning himself right next to Jason in the limo, Rev. Faith began reading scripture aloud, "Your word have I hidden in my heart that I might not sin against Thee…No temptation has come upon you except that which is common to man…the Lord always provides a way of escape…I love the Lord, He heard my cry."

"Ow!" Jason blurted out in acute pain from being pinched in his right side. Sasha was obviously trying to get his attention. Keeping one eye on Rev. Faith sitting on his left, Jason inconspicuously leaned his right ear as close to Sasha as possible. *Keep your cool, Baby*, he thought.

"Jay, it's like God is right here in the limo. Since when does God ride in limos with two levels?" Sasha whispered.

"I guess God wanted to step out in style tonight." The upside down, half-moon turned right-side-up and Sasha leaned back with a smile. She nudged him in his side, causing him to rock into Rev. Faith, who was so engrossed in reading, he didn't seem to notice.

"Pardon me," the driver broke the recitation over the speaker. "In a moment, a couple of passengers will be joining us. Take note of the ceiling door. Master Jason, please do us the honor of pushing the release button on the remote control to lower the stairs."

After looking around at each other, everyone shifted to make room for the stairs. Miss Teach finished her pina colada and handed Jason the remote.

One push of a button unlocked a mini-flight of stairs with five steps that smoothly lowered. In a flash, the driver was ringing someone else's door-bell and five kids jumped down the stairs and bolted toward the limo door. Into the limo and up the ceiling stairs they climbed, laughing, joking and claiming the limo as their own.

"Who are those kids, yo?" Jason asked bewilderedly.

"Those are kids from the community center. Well, they attend the programs at the community center, but they live in the orphanage."

"They live in an *orphanage*?" said Sasha.

"Yes. Some of the students at our school go to the orphanage to tutor them after school and this year they wanted to go to the prom."

Miss Teach was misty, "Isn't that lovely! Does any one have a tissue," she sniffled.

"Rev. Faith, I don't get it," Jason admitted with wrinkles in his forehead, "why do these kids want to go to our prom? We don't know them."

"Believe me, these kids know you. They've been watching you for two years now. Jason, they've seen you play basketball each season and they are always talking about how smart and beautiful Sasha is."

"When did those kids even see me? I'm not an athlete or anything." Sasha was just as confused as Jason.

Miss Teach had to chime in, "Sasha, kids are always watching and looking up to older kids. You may not notice them, but they always take note of you. Sometimes they take to you just because they like something about you."

"Miss Teach is right, Sasha. These kids were there for the fashion show fundraiser your class held last year. They were special greeters that night. All of them, especially the girls, were in awe of you when they saw you walk down the runway. From that day on, they wanted to be like Miss Sasha."

"Wow! I never even saw them," said Sasha in utter amazement. Her younger brother and their friends never acted like they paid her any attention, but everything Rev. Faith and Miss Teach said was really getting to her. She never saw herself as a role model for anyone before.

"Master Jason," said the driver interrupting Sasha's thoughts, "please secure the stairs with the remote before we travel to our final destination." Jason wasn't convinced he was the master of anything, but he sure liked having control of the remote.

Sasha, Jason, Miss Teach, Rev. Faith, the five ten-year olds and the driver continued on their unending journey to the prom. Finally settling into the idea that she was not going to the prom alone with her date, Sasha turned up the music volume and joined the kids on the top level.

As Sasha looked out the windows with the kids, she noticed that her surroundings looked familiar. In ten minutes, she watched the vehicle pull up into her aunt's driveway. Skipping down the steps, Sasha curiously followed the driver to the door. Before he could even reach out his hand to ring the bell, her aunt opened the door and yelled, "Surprise!"

Sasha's birthday was months ago! Was her aunt going senile already? The driver tripped into the doorway as Sasha's aunt pulled him into the house. When Sasha entered the house and looked up, she saw her mother, father, two aunts and two cousins all decked out and ready to go.

"Let me guess: They're all going with us, right?" Sasha asked almost rhetorically. The driver insisted on answering, "Yes, Princess Sasha. They are all going with you to your prom."

"Baby, girl, I love you so much," her mother began with tears, "and I just want the best for you. We are your family and we will always be with you wherever you go."

"That's right," her father chimed in, "you can't get rid of us—we're a part of your genes."

Sasha's aunt, Carol, grabbed her and gave her a big hug. "Wherever you go, you represent us. We will be there with you tonight at prom because when people see you, they see us" she said with a warm grin.

"Well, I just want to go because I like to dance!" said Little Leslie, her cousin.

Cousin Britanna added, "Me, too—and I want to see all the cute boys!"

Slightly overwhelmed by it all, Sasha assured Britanna there would be plenty of boys there and made sure she said, "The prom isn't just about being with boys or being noticed by them. It's about everyone having a good time in a safe environment." Her cousins weren't quite buying that. Sasha put her arms around Little Leslie and Britanna as they all walked toward the limo.

Just before the limo pulled off for its final destination, Sasha returned to her seat next to Jason and he took her hand. Sasha leaned over to him with a smile and said, "Jay, I'm glad the limo company recognized that we needed room for all these people."

"Me, too. This has been crazy! Sasha, I really wanted our time in the limo to be special—just me and you, you know?" Jason slightly whined.

"I know—I did, too. The limo driver wasn't lying; this really was a long journey!

"Well, I just really wanted to make you feel special and I thought if we made out and got our groove on between home and the prom, all of your fantasies would come true. I love you, girl. I want you to be happy."

With her index finger on his lips, Sasha quieted Jason and let him know she really was alright with all that happened to interrupt their previous plans. It took this long journey for her to understand respect, honor, dignity and happiness. All of the people in the limo had contributed something significant to her life and even if they had not gotten in the limo, there would be traces of them in her heart, mind, thoughts and actions.

"Jay, when I look around, I see people who really care about me — even God. This ride has blown my mind even better than you could!"

My Prom Passions: The Ride of a Lifetime

1. Who are the special people in my life and why?

2. How might my actions on prom night be interpreted by people who identify me as a role model?

3. How will I make prom night choices that will reflect and respect the special people in my life?

—*For Young Women Who Want More*—

Have you noticed how easily we can switch up when we think no one else will find out? If we think we'll get away with it, we'll act differently on our special night than we normally would around family or other influential people in our lives. However, no matter where we are, our identity still remains the same: you are always you. So, prom night isn't a time to switch identities or throw common sense out the window.

No matter where you go, what you believe is one of those identity shapers that should influence your actions. Not only do your beliefs about life matter, but so do your religious beliefs. If you're not going to adhere to your beliefs on prom night, what's the point in having them in the first place? Your beliefs should help you select your prom date and decide how to conduct yourself on the night of the event. Your world view and faith are important because they speak to who you are: don't live contrary to what you say you believe. *Your beliefs concerning life and faith are integral parts of your life, not meant to be ignored or forgotten on prom night.*

Like beliefs, family grounds us in our identity. Like it or not, what you do on prom night will reflect upon your family. If everyone based your family's reputation on the way you carry yourself at prom and after prom, what would be said of your family? Listen to your family's instruction to be careful, to return home on time, to call when required, to avoid certain places. These cautions are meant to protect you from things you can't imagine ever happening to you.

-Listen, my [daughter] to your father's instruction and do not forsake your mother's teaching.-
Proverb 1:8

Chapter 7

*F*inally!

If you've read each chapter, answered the questions and stepped up to the challenges presented in this book, you are well on your way to experiencing the night of your life! Prom can be all about fulfilling your prom passions; you just want to make sure your passions will lead you to the best destination.

Again, here are the six keys to making prom your best night ever:

1. Identify and plan for the prom memories you want to have

Nikki, Aaliyah and Sarah all woke up the morning after prom with memories—some to be cherished forever and others they'd rather forget. Prom doesn't have to simply happen to you: you can and should plan for the memories you want of prom. Consequences do come as a result of our actions, so remember to consider "life after prom" as you envision your perfect night.

2. *Create a financial plan to finance your prom evening*

Each of the girls in this chapter had to find a way to pay for prom. Kristin's father immediately agreed to pay for prom. However, Tracy and Jessica had to negotiate with their parents. Prom isn't all about money, but finances are a crucial issue that should be addressed as early as possible. Creating a budget and financial timeline are essential. Remember, a little creativity goes a long way!

3. *Think for yourself—know who or what is influencing you*

Thinking isn't automatic in a world where you are constantly bombarded with messages telling you what to want. Messages, family history, peer pressure and faulty reasoning can all tamper with your sense of identity. You owe it to yourself to find out the truth, the whole truth and nothing but the truth, so you can make the best decisions possible.

4. *Be true to the cry of your heart*

You can be true to yourself! Many betray themselves by giving in to the pressure to have sex, by being sexually active or lowering their personal standards on prom night. You must determine the difference between "this is me" and "this is not me" so you can identify and be cautious of the boundary between respect and disrespect. Others will test every boundary you claim to have, but maintaining the boundaries you set is well worth the struggle. You don't have to have sex on prom night—whether you are a virgin or one who has had sex before.

5. *Construct your world with the best materials*
We all create our own worlds in which we feel safe. Sometimes our worlds are so twisted we don't know why we act the way we do. Perhaps you need to recreate your world with a new set of standards and more edifying ways of thinking and behaving. Create your world with love, complete truth and a positive self-image instead of self-hate, faulty reasoning or negativity. You deserve to enjoy life without harming yourself or others.

6. *Remember your identity and who you represent*
Tasha and Jason experienced a most unusual ride to the prom. They never expected to share their limo with a teacher, school chaplain, five orphans or family members; however, in the end, they had the ride of their lives. No matter where we go, our identity, beliefs and family reputation travel with us. You never know who is watching or looking up to you. Remember the awareness issues raised in school, the moral lessons taught in your place of worship and the rules your family has set: these things may very well protect and save your life.

Your best night is here!

*A*bout *T*he *A*uthor

—⊰◈⊱—

Joy **Singleton** is dedicated to empowering youth and young adults. An ordained minister, author and speaker, she is currently Pastor of Young Adult Ministry at Cathedral International, Perth Amboy, NJ. Some of her writings can be found on www.theuncommonlife.com and www.iansweredthecall.com. Joy received her Master of Divinity degree from Princeton Theological Seminary.

At the age of eighteen, Joy gave her life to Christ as a freshman at Howard University, where she received a full academic scholarship. During her junior year, she was licensed to the gospel ministry at the age of twenty years old. Joy faithfully seeks to fulfill her commission to be an encouragement to others and to be both a positive and godly example of excellence.

To Contact The Author Write:
Joy Singleton
P.O. Box 7517
North Brunswick, NJ 08902-7517
prompassions@aol.com

Printed in the United States
52123LVS00001B/316-414